Hansen

illustration **nancy speir**
written by **wallace c. wadsworth**

Dalmatian Press

One day Henny Penny went into the woods to search for nuts. A big acorn fell from a tree and hit her feathered head.

"Cut-cut-cut-cut!" squawked poor Henny Penny. "Oh, goodness! The sky's a falling, surely! I must go and tell the King!" She thought he ought to know about it.

So she hurried along, and in a little while she met Ducky Lucky.

"Quack!Quack!" called Ducky Lucky. "Good morning, Henny Penny, where are you going this fine day?"

"Oh, deary me, Ducky Lucky!" cried Henny Penny. "I was in the woods gathering nuts, and a piece of the sky fell on my feathered head. I'm going to tell the King the sky's a-falling!"

"Oh!, what a dreadful thing! Quack! Quack!"
exclaimed Ducky Lucky. "May I come along with
you?" "Certainly," said Henny Penny. "We'll both
go and tell the King."

So they hurried along, and whom should they
meet but Goosey Loosey.

"Honk! Honk!" called out Goosey Loosey."
"Where are the two of you going this fine day?"

"Oh, deary me, Goosey Loosey!" cried Ducky
Lucky. "Henny Penny was in the woods gathering
nuts, and a piece of the sky fell upon her
feathered head. We're on our way to tell the
King the sky's a-falling."

"Oh, what a dreadful thing! Honk! Honk!" exclaimed Goosey Loosey. "May I come along with you?" "Certainly," said Ducky Lucky. "All three of us will go and tell the King."

So they hurried along, and whom should they meet but Gander Lander. "Squonk! Squonk!" called Gander Lander. "Where are the three of you going this fine day?"

"Oh, deary me, Gander Lander!" cried Goosey
Loosey. "Henny Penny was in the woods gathering
nuts, and a piece of the sky fell upon her
feathered head. We're on our way to tell
the King the sky's a-falling."

"Oh, what a dreadful thing! Squonk! Squonk!" exclaimed Gander Lander. "May I come along with you?"

"Certainly," said Goosey Loosey. "All four of us will go and tell the King."

So they all hurried along, and whom should them meet but Turkey Lurkey.

"Gobble! Gobble!" called Turkey Lurkey, stretching out his long neck. "where are the four of you going this fine day?"

"Oh, deary me, Turkey Lurkey!" cried Gander Lander. Henny Penny was in the woods gathering nuts, and a piece of sky fell upon her feathered head. We're on our way to tell the King the sky's a-falling."

"Oh, what a dreadful thing! Gobble! Gobble!"
exclaimed Turkey Lurkey. "May I come along
with you?"

"Certainly," said Gander Lander. "All five of us
will go and tell the King."

So they hurried along, and whom should they
meet but Foxy Loxy!

"Good morning to you, my pretty friends,"
called Foxy Loxy, smiling slyly upon them all.
"Where are the five of you going this fine day?"

"Oh, deary me, Foxy Loxy!" cried Turkey Lurkey.
"Henny Penny was in the woods gathering nuts,
and a piece of the sky fell upon her feathered head.
We're on our way to tell the King the sky's a-falling."

"Oh, what a dreadful thing!" exclaimed Foxy Loxy, but he smiled as though it might not be such a dreadful thing, after all. "Was Henny Penny standing near the big oak tree at the edge of the woods, may I ask?"

"That was just the place!"cried Henny Penny.

"Ah, I thought so,"said Foxy Loxy. "I was there yesterday, and I thought the sky looked rather weak. The King should know about it. Are you sure that you know the way to the palace?"

The friends all looked at each other and shook their heads.

"Then I shall lead you to it'" said Foxy Loxy, and he licked his lips hungrily. "Just follow me, and we'll all go and tell the King the sky's a-falling."

So Foxy Loxy led the way, and they soon came to a big hole that went beneath the roots of a tree.

Now this was really the door to Foxy Loxy's den, but he smiled and said, "This is a short way to the King's palace. I shall go in first, and you must follow me, one at a time. Then you will be in the presence of the King, to tell him the sky's a-falling."

Henny Penny and her friends promised to do just as he said. Foxy Loxy smiled slyly, and led the way into his burrow.

There he waited, thinking of what a fine dinner Henny Penny and her friends would make.

Henny Penny started toward the big hole.

Then, all at once, she remembered something.

"Oh goodness me!" she cried, "I have forgotten to lay my egg today! There are enough of you to go and tell the King without me."

Away went Henny Penny as fast as she could go. Ducky Lucky and Goosey Loosey and Gander Lander and Turkey Lurkey watched her go.

"Foxy Loxy knows the way to the King's palace," said Goosey Loosey. "Let him tell the King the sky's a-falling. I have my work to do, and I must get back to it at once."

"So must we," said all the others, and away
they hurried.

Foxy Loxy waited hungrily for Henny Penny and her friends to come. After a while he came out to look for them. But they were gone, every one of them-Henny Penny and Ducky Lucky and Goosey Loosey and Gander Lander and Turkey Lurkey!

And so it was that sly Foxy Loxy had to go without his fine dinner and the King was never told that the sky was falling.

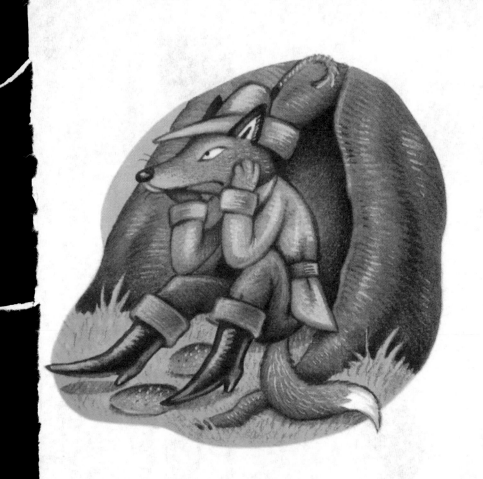

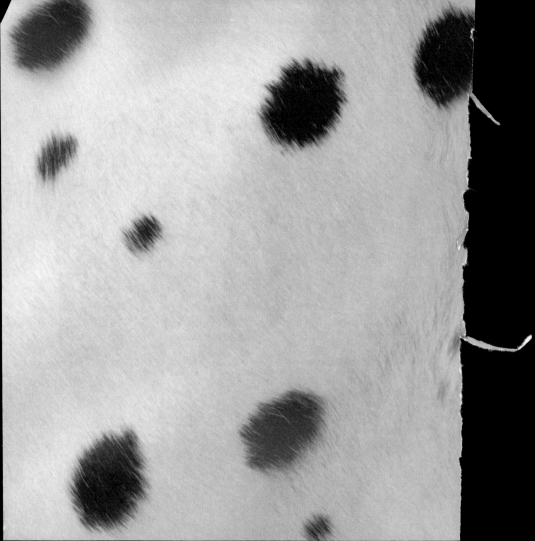